1967

This book may be kept

FOURTEEN DAYS

A fine will be charged for each day the book is kept overtime.

GAYLORD 142   PRINTED IN U.S.A.

LUPERCAL

by the same author

*

THE HAWK IN THE RAIN

LUPERCAL

✤

TED HUGHES

HARPER & BROTHERS

Publishers

New York

LUPERCAL
copyright © 1960 by Ted Hughes

Printed in Great Britain

ACKNOWLEDGMENTS

Some of these poems have appeared in *The Atlantic Monthly*, *Audience*, *The Critical Quarterly*, *Encounter*, *The Grecourt Review*, *The Guinness Book of Poetry 1960*, *Harper's Magazine*, *The Hudson Review*, *The London Magazine*, *Mademoiselle*, *The Massachusetts Review*, *Nation*, *New Poems 1958*, *New Poems 1959*, *The New Statesman*, *Northern Broadsheet*, *The Observer*, *The Paris Review*, *The Partisan Review*, *The Poetry Supplement* (Poetry Book Society, London: Christmas 1957), *Poetry* (Chicago), *Poetry from Cambridge 1958*, *The Sewanee Review*, *The Spectator*, *The Times Literary Supplement*. The following poems originally appeared in *The New Yorker:* Bullfrog, Esther's Tomcat (under the title "Tomcat"). Acknowledgment is made also to the John Simon Guggenheim Memorial Foundation.

CONTENTS

7

CONTENTS

THINGS PRESENT

All things being done or undone
As my hands adore or abandon—
Embody a now, erect a here
A bare-backed tramp and a ditch without fire

Cat or bread; and no shoes,
Honour, or hope, him—whose
Progenitors back to the sea-salt
Bride-bed to cradle assoiled

Honour of its shifty eyes, and hope
Of its shaky heart-beat, and step
By step got into stout shoes beneath
A roof treed to deflect death.

My sires had towers and great names,
And that their effort be brought to an edge
Honed their bodies away, dreams
The tramp in the sodden ditch.

EVERYMAN'S ODYSSEY

Telemachus, now to remember your coming of age.
Years your trust was open as the doors of your house
To the boisterous princes, all so phrasing your mother,
So cushioning the going of her feet with the glow of their eyes,
Who brought such trinkets, and hoisted the jugglers and the
    dancers
Onto the protesting trestles of your tables.

Your mother, white, a woe freezing a silence,
Parried long their impertinence with her shuttle,
And such after-banquet belching of adulation
Through your hoop and handball years. O Telemachus
Remember the day you saw the spears on the wall
And their great blades shook light at you like the sea.

If these memories move at all in your ghost
This last must open up a wound: recall that year
You sulked among the suitors—too big for their comfort
And yet too few for their fear. Your father's honour
Was a sword in the scabbard of your body you could not draw,
What patience you had a slow bird quartering the seas.

But avenge yourself on recalling that. I would hear
How the father arrives out of the bottom of the world.
I would see one of the beggars that brawl on my porch
Reach hands to the bow hardly to be strung by man—
I would see these gluttons, guests by grace of their numbers,
Flung through the doors with their bellies full of arrows.

MAYDAY ON HOLDERNESS

This evening, motherly summer moves in the pond.
I look down into the decomposition of leaves—
The furnace door whirling with larvae.

From Hull's sunset smudge
Humber is melting eastward, my south skyline:
A loaded single vein, it drains
The effort of the inert North—Sheffield's ores,
Bog pools, dregs of toadstools, tributary
Graves, dunghills, kitchens, hospitals.
The unkillable North Sea swallows it all.
Insects, drunken, drop out of the air.
Birth-soils,
The sea-salts, scoured me, cortex and intestine,
To receive these remains.
As the incinerator, as the sun,
As the spider, I had a whole world in my hands.
Flowerlike, I loved nothing.
Dead and unborn are in God comfortable.
What a length of gut is growing and breathing—
This mute eater, biting through the mind's
Nursery floor, with eel and hyena and vulture,
With creepy-crawly and the root,
With the sea-worm, entering its birthright.

The stars make pietas. The owl announces its sanity.

The crow sleeps glutted and the stoat begins.
There are eye-guarded eggs in the hedgerows,
Hot haynests under the roots in burrows.
Couples at their pursuits are laughing in the lanes.

The North Sea lies soundless. Beneath it
Smoulder the wars: to heart-beats, bomb, bayonet.
"Mother, Mother!" cries the pierced helmet.
Cordite oozings of Gallipoli,

Curded to beastings, broached my palate,
The expressionless gaze of the leopard,
The coils of the sleeping anaconda,
The nightlong frenzy of shrews.

FEBRUARY

The wolf with its belly stitched full of big pebbles;
Nibelung wolves barbed like black pineforest
Against a red sky, over blue snow; or that long grin
Above the tucked coverlet—none suffice.

A photograph: the hairless, knuckled feet
Of the last wolf killed in Britain spoiled him for wolves:
The worst since has been so much mere Alsatian.
Now it is the dream cries "Wolf!" where these feet

Print the moonlit doorstep, or run and run
Through the hush of parkland, bodiless, headless;
With small seeming of inconvenience
By day, too, pursue, siege all thought;

Bring him to an abrupt poring stop
Over engravings of gibbet-hung wolves,
As at a cage where the scraggy Spanish wolf
Danced, smiling, brown eyes doggily begging

A ball to be thrown. These feet, deprived,
Disdaining all that are caged, or storied, or pictured,
Through and throughout the true world search
For their vanished head, for the world

Vanished with the head, the teeth, the quick eyes——.
Now, lest they choose his head,
Under severe moons he sits making
Wolf-masks, mouths clamped well onto the world.

CROW HILL

The farms are oozing craters in
Sheer sides under the sodden moors:
When it is not wind it is rain,
Neither of which will stop at doors:
One will damp beds and the other shake
Dreams beneath sleep it cannot break.

Between the weather and the rock
Farmers make a little heat;
Cows that sway a bony back,
Pigs upon delicate feet
Hold off the sky, trample the strength
That shall level these hills at length.

Buttoned from the blowing mist
Walk the ridges of ruined stone.
What humbles these hills has raised
The arrogance of blood and bone,
And thrown the hawk upon the wind,
And lit the fox in the dripping ground.

A WOMAN UNCONSCIOUS

Russia and America circle each other;
Threats nudge an act that were without doubt
A melting of the mould in the mother,
Stones melting about the root.

The quick of the earth burned out:
The toil of all our ages a loss
With leaf and insect. Yet flitting thought
(Not to be thought ridiculous)

Shies from the world-cancelling black
Of its playing shadow: it has learned
That there's no trusting (trusting to luck)
Dates when the world's due to be burned;

That the future's no calamitous change
But a malingering of now,
Histories, towns, faces that no
Malice or accident much derange.

And though bomb be matched against bomb,
Though all mankind wince out and nothing endure—
Earth gone in an instant flare—
Did a lesser death come

Onto the white hospital bed
Where one, numb beyond her last of sense,
Closed her eyes on the world's evidence
And into pillows sunk her head.

STRAWBERRY HILL

A stoat danced on the lawns here
To the music of the maskers;
Drinking the staring hare dry, bit
Through grammar and corset. They nailed to a door

The stoat with the sun in its belly,
But its red unmanageable life
Has licked the stylist out of their skulls,
Has sucked that age like an egg and gone off

Along ditches where flies and leaves
Overpower our tongues, got into some grave—
Not a dog to follow it down—
Emerges, thirsting, in far Asia, in Brixton.

DICK STRAIGHTUP

Past eighty, but never in eighty years—
Eighty winters on the windy ridge
Of England—has he buttoned his shirt or his jacket.
He sits in the bar-room seat he has been
Polishing with his backside sixty-odd years
Where nobody else sits. White is his head,
But his cheek high, hale as when he emptied
Every Saturday the twelve-pint tankard at a tilt,
Swallowed the whole serving of thirty eggs,
And banged the big bass drum for Heptonstall—
With a hundred other great works, still talked of.
Age has stiffened him, but not dazed or bent,
The blue eye has come clear of time:
At a single pint, now, his memory sips slowly,
His belly strong as a tree bole.

He survives among hills, nourished by stone and height.
The dust of Achilles and Cuchulain
Itches in the palms of scholars; thin clerks exercise
In their bed-sitters at midnight, and the meat salesman can
Loft fully four hundred pounds. But this one,
With no more application than sitting,
And drinking, and singing, fell in the sleet, late,
Dammed the pouring gutter; and slept there; and, throughout
A night searched by shouts and lamps, froze,
Grew to the road with welts of ice. He was chipped out at dawn
Warm as a pie and snoring.

The gossip of men younger by forty years—
Loud in his company since he no longer says much—

Empties, refills and empties their glasses.
Or their strenuous silence places the dominoes
(That are old as the house) into patterns
Gone with the game; the darts that glint to the dartboard
Pin no remarkable instant. The young men sitting
Taste their beer as by imitation,
Borrow their words as by impertinence
Because he sits there so full of legend and life
Quiet as a man alone.

He lives with sixty and seventy years ago,
And of everything he knows three quarters is in the grave,
Or tumbled down, or vanished. To be understood
His words must tug up the bottom-most stones of this village,
This clutter of blackstone gulleys, peeping curtains,
And a graveyard bigger and deeper than the village
That sways in the tide of wind and rain some fifty
Miles off the Irish sea.
                              The lamp above the pub-door
Wept yellow when he went out and the street
Of spinning darkness roared like a machine
As the wind applied itself. His upright walk,
His strong back, I commemorate now,
And his white blown head going out between a sky and an
    earth
That were bundled into placeless blackness, the one
Company of his mind.

Obit.

Now, you are strong as the earth you have entered.

This is a birthplace picture. Green into blue
The hills run deep and limpid. The weasel's
Berry-eyed red lock-head, gripping the dream
That holds good, goes lost in the heaved calm

Of the earth you have entered.

FOURTH OF JULY

The hot shallows and seas we bring our blood from
Slowly dwindled; cooled
To sewage estuary, to trout-stocked tarn.
Even the Amazon's taxed and patrolled

To set laws by the few jaws—
Piranha and jaguar.
Columbus' huckstering breath
Blew inland through North America

Killing the last of the mammoths.
The right maps have no monsters.
Now the mind's wandering elementals,
Ousted from their traveller-told

Unapproachable islands,
From their heavens and their burning underworld,
Wait dully at the traffic crossing,
Or lean over headlines, taking nothing in.

A DREAM OF HORSES

We were born grooms, in stable-straw we sleep still,
All our wealth horse-dung and the combings of horses,
And all we can talk about is what horses ail.

Out of the night that gulfed beyond the palace-gate
There shook hooves and hooves and hooves of horses:
Our horses battered their stalls; their eyes jerked white.

And we ran out, mice in our pockets and straw in our hair,
Into darkness that was avalanching to horses
And a quake of hooves. Our lantern's little orange flare

Made a round mask of our each sleep-dazed face,
Bodiless, or else bodied by horses
That whinnied and bit and cannoned the world from its place.

The tall palace was so white, the moon was so round,
Everything else this plunging of horses
To the rim of our eyes that strove for the shapes of the sound.

We crouched at our lantern, our bodies drank the din,
And we longed for a death trampled by such horses
As every grain of the earth had hooves and mane.

We must have fallen like drunkards into a dream
Of listening, lulled by the thunder of the horses.
We awoke stiff; broad day had come.

Out through the gate the unprinted desert stretched
To stone and scorpion; our stable-horses
Lay in their straw, in a hag-sweat, listless and wretched.

Now let us, tied, be quartered by these poor horses,
If but doomsday's flames be great horses,
The forever itself a circling of the hooves of horses.

ESTHER'S TOMCAT

Daylong this tomcat lies stretched flat
As an old rough mat, no mouth and no eyes.
Continual wars and wives are what
Have tattered his ears and battered his head.

Like a bundle of old rope and iron
Sleeps till blue dusk. Then reappear
His eyes, green as ringstones: he yawns wide red,
Fangs fine as a lady's needle and bright.

A tomcat sprang at a mounted knight,
Locked round his neck like a trap of hooks
While the knight rode fighting its clawing and bite.
After hundreds of years the stain's there

On the stone where he fell, dead of the tom:
That was at Barnborough. The tomcat still
Grallochs odd dogs on the quiet,
Will take the head clean off your simple pullet,

Is unkillable. From the dog's fury,
From gunshot fired point-blank he brings
His skin whole, and whole
From owlish moons of bekittenings

Among ashcans. He leaps and lightly
Walks upon sleep, his mind on the moon.
Nightly over the round world of men,
Over the roofs go his eyes and outcry.

HISTORIAN

As if the eye and the head
Were an underworld, all the dead
Come to garrulous quarters there,
Dignifying at a live ear

What befell. Each (his pride,
His downright lying vanity being
Disembodied from any twice-doing
That could prove, as from blood

That could blush) can brag
The decisive random of chance
Was concealed skill of his choice, license
Word breathed into a wig

To raze like Attila. Back and forth,
Vociferous as when they lived,
Infuriated still to be braved
Each by the rest, they protest their worth

And winnings of this world. Their graves
Have devoured tenure; perhaps something
Grafted to a warm bone's darkness lives
Of their effort, but to bring

Them to claim, still, clear gains
On times and bodies they have long lost
Takes a frivolous advocate. Or a live brain's
Envying to master and last.

PENNINES IN APRIL

If this county were a sea (that is solid rock
Deeper than any sea) these hills heaving
Out of the east, mass behind mass, at this height
Hoisting heather and stones to the sky
Must burst upwards and topple into Lancashire.

Perhaps, as the earth turns, such ground-stresses
Do come rolling westward through the locked land.
Now, measuring the miles of silence
Your eye takes the strain: through

Landscapes gliding blue as water
Those barrellings of strength are heaving slowly and heave
To your feet and surf upwards
In a still, fiery air, hauling the imagination,
Carrying the larks upward.

HAWK ROOSTING

I sit in the top of the wood, my eyes closed.
Inaction, no falsifying dream
Between my hooked head and hooked feet:
Or in sleep rehearse perfect kills and eat.

The convenience of the high trees!
The air's buoyancy and the sun's ray
Are of advantage to me;
And the earth's face upward for my inspection.

My feet are locked upon the rough bark.
It took the whole of Creation
To produce my foot, my each feather:
Now I hold Creation in my foot

Or fly up, and revolve it all slowly—
I kill where I please because it is all mine.
There is no sophistry in my body:
My manners are tearing off heads—

The allotment of death.
For the one path of my flight is direct
Through the bones of the living.
No arguments assert my right:

The sun is behind me.
Nothing has changed since I began.
My eye has permitted no change.
I am going to keep things like this.

NICHOLAS FERRER

Brought to bare trees, to spike and shard
Browned by cold, our birds
Breast a homing departure; on wings press
To correct earth's sure tilt into darkness

By a practical move—though they are more
Ignorant than their charted bones,
On lighthouse comforts beat out their brains,
In the Atlantic holes tire—

Toward an estranged sun. Rain-logged, wind-unroofed,
The manor farm hulked its last use
As landmark. The mice survived
All ownership, contested the house

With the owls, and toadstools
Heaved the black pavement of the kitchen. No
Signature but this threshold-held hollow
Remained of some vigorous souls

That had Englished for Elizabeth. Pigs and hay
Filled a church oozing manure mud
From the porch when Nicholas, with all his family,
Alit here, entering the shroud

Of weather and dissolution. That day on,
The farm, the church and Nicholas' frontal bone
Walled out a clouded world: he housekept
In fire of the martyrs: there the tree that crabbed

In Cromwell's belly as it bloomed in Rome
Burned down to the blue calm
They called God's look, and through years illumed
Their fingers on the bibles, and gleamed

From the eagle of brass.
                                    Stones and grass
Have sealed our vows. Pig-sties, the earthen face
Drink November. And again the fire of God
Is under the shut heart, under the grave sod.

TO PAINT A WATER LILY

A green level of lily leaves
Roofs the pond's chamber and paves

The flies' furious arena: study
These, the two minds of this lady.

First observe the air's dragonfly
That eats meat, that bullets by

Or stands in space to take aim;
Others as dangerous comb the hum

Under the trees. There are battle-shouts
And death-cries everywhere hereabouts

But inaudible, so the eyes praise
To see the colours of these flies

Rainbow their arcs, spark, or settle
Cooling like beads of molten metal

Through the spectrum. Think what worse
Is the pond-bed's matter of course;

Prehistoric bedragonned times
Crawl that darkness with Latin names,

Have evolved no improvements there,
Jaws for heads, the set stare,

Ignorant of age as of hour—
Now paint the long-necked lily-flower

Which, deep in both worlds, can be still
As a painting, trembling hardly at all

Though the dragonfly alight,
Whatever horror nudge her root.

URN BURIAL

Born to these gentle stones and grass,
The whole of himself to himself:
Cheek by jowl in with the weasel;
Caesar no ghost but his passion.

An improvement on the eagle's hook,
The witty spider competitor,
Sets his word's strength against the rock,
No foot wrong in the dance figure—

So by manners, by music, to abash
The wretch of death that stands in his shoes:
The aping shape of earth—sure
Of its weight now as in future.

OF CATS

A heart constituted wholly of cats
(Even as the family nose derives)
From father and mother a child inherits,
And every cat gets fully nine lives.

Wildest cats, with scruff cats, queenly cats
(Crowned), they jig to violins; they go stately
Where a torched pageantry celebrates
A burial, or crowning (of a cat); or sing sweetly

At your ears and in harmony left with right
Till the moon bemoods: to the new, to the full,
Only look up: possessing night—
Cattic Bacchanal! A world of wild lamps and wauling,

A world gone to the cats, every cat of the heart out,
And darkness and light a cat upon a cat——.
They have outwitted our nimblest wits.
One who, one night, sank a cat in a sack

With a stone to the canal-bottom
(Under the bridge, in the very belly of the black)
And hurried a mile home
Found that cat on the doorstep waiting for him.

So are we all held in utter mock by the cats.

FIRE-EATER

Those stars are the fleshed forebears
Of these dark hills, bowed like labourers,

And of my blood.

The death of a gnat is a star's mouth: its skin,
Like Mary's or Semele's, thin

As the skin of fire:
A star fell on her, a sun devoured her.

My appetite is good
Now to manage both Orion and Dog

With a mouthful of earth, my staple.
Worm-sort, root-sort, going where it is profitable.

A star pierces the slug,

The tree is caught up in the constellations.
My skull burrows among antennae and fronds.

ACROBATS

Among ropes and dark heights
Spot-lights sparkle those silver postures:
(The trapeze beginning to swing)
Casually they lean out
Over eyes opened deeper
Than the floored drop. Then fling
Out onto nothing, snap, jerk
Fulcrumed without fail
On axes immaterial as
Only geometry should use.

None below in the dumbstruck crowd
Thinks it else but miracle
That a man go somersaulting
(As might hardly be dared in the head)
Bodily out on space,
Gibboning, bird-vaulting
Out of all sedentary belief,
With unearthly access of grace,
Of ease: freer firmer world found
A hundred feet above ground.

The crowd, holding to their seats hard
Under the acrobats' hurtle and arc,
In their hearts miming that daring,
Are no longer assured
Of their body's nonchalant pride
Or of earth's firmness, bearing
Plunge of that high risk without
That flight; with only a dread
Crouching to get away from these
On its hands and knees.

34

The acrobats flashed
Above earth's ancient inertia,
Faltering of the will,
And the dullness of flesh—
In the dream's orbit; shone, soared,
Mocking vigil and ordeal,
And the prayer of long attempting
Body had endured
To break from a hard-held trembling seat
And soar at that height.

THE GOOD LIFE

Nothing of profit to be got
So poor-bare to wind and to rain,
His spirit gone to patch his boot,
The hermit returned to the world again.

"Revelation's a burden not to be borne
Save by square-shouldered self-respect."
But when that latter jaunted bedecked
His vanity was of apparent horn.

"Quiet enough at last I have won,
My body relieved of rag and of ache:
Only a plump, cuffed citizen
Gets enough quiet to hear God speak."

Loud he prayed then; but late or early
Never a murmur came to his need
Save "I'd be delighted!" and "Yours sincerely",
And "Thank you very much indeed!"

THE BULL MOSES

A hoist up and I could lean over
The upper edge of the high half-door,
My left foot ledged on the hinge, and look in at the byre's
Blaze of darkness: a sudden shut-eyed look
Backward into the head.
                                    Blackness is depth
Beyond star. But the warm weight of his breathing,
The ammoniac reek of his litter, the hotly-tongued
Mash of his cud, steamed against me.
Then, slowly, as onto the mind's eye—
The brow like masonry, the deep-keeled neck:
Something come up there onto the brink of the gulf,
Hadn't heard of the world, too deep in itself to be called to,
Stood in sleep. He would swing his muzzle at a fly
But the square of sky where I hung, shouting, waving,
Was nothing to him; nothing of our light
Found any reflection in him.
                                    Each dusk the farmer led him
Down to the pond to drink and smell the air,
And he took no pace but the farmer
Led him to take it, as if he knew nothing
Of the ages and continents of his fathers,
Shut, while he wombed, to a dark shed
And steps between his door and the duckpond;
The weight of the sun and the moon and the world hammered
To a ring of brass through his nostrils.
                                    He would raise
His streaming muzzle and look out over the meadows,

But the grasses whispered nothing awake, the fetch
Of the distance drew nothing to momentum
In the locked black of his powers. He came strolling gently
    back,
Paused neither toward the pig-pens on his right,
Nor toward the cow-byres on his left: something
Deliberate in his leisure, some beheld future
Founding in his quiet.
                    I kept the door wide,
Closed it after him and pushed the bolt.

CAT AND MOUSE

On the sheep-cropped summit, under hot sun,
The mouse crouched, staring out the chance
It dared not take.
                    Time and a world
Too old to alter, the five mile prospect—
Woods, villages, farms—hummed its heat-heavy
Stupor of life.
                    Whether to two
Feet or four, how are prayers contracted!
Whether in God's eye or the eye of a cat.

VIEW OF A PIG

The pig lay on a barrow dead.
It weighed, they said, as much as three men.
Its eyes closed, pink white eyelashes.
Its trotters stuck straight out.

Such weight and thick pink bulk
Set in death seemed not just dead.
It was less than lifeless, further off.
It was like a sack of wheat.

I thumped it without feeling remorse.
One feels guilty insulting the dead,
Walking on graves. But this pig
Did not seem able to accuse.

It was too dead. Just so much
A poundage of lard and pork.
Its last dignity had entirely gone.
It was not a figure of fun.

Too dead now to pity.
To remember its life, din, stronghold
Of earthly pleasure as it had been,
Seemed a false effort, and off the point.

Too deadly factual. Its weight
Oppressed me—how could it be moved?
And the trouble of cutting it up!
The gash in its throat was shocking, but not pathetic.

Once I ran at a fair in the noise
To catch a greased piglet
That was faster and nimbler than a cat,
Its squeal was the rending of metal.

Pigs must have hot blood, they feel like ovens.
Their bite is worse than a horse's—
They chop a half-moon clean out.
They eat cinders, dead cats.

Distinctions and admirations such
As this one was long finished with.
I stared at it a long time. They were going to scald it,
Scald it and scour it like a doorstep.

THE RETIRED COLONEL

Who lived at the top end of our street
Was a Mafeking stereotype, ageing.
Came, face pulped scarlet with kept rage,
For air past our gate.
Barked at his dog knout and whipcrack
And cowerings of India: five or six wars
Stiffened in his reddened neck;
Brow bull-down for the stroke.

Wife dead, daughters gone, lived on
Honouring his own caricature.
Shot through the heart with whisky wore
The lurch like ancient courage, would not go **down**
While posterity's trash stood, held
His habits like a last stand, even
As if he had Victoria rolled
In a Union Jack in that stronghold.

And what if his sort should vanish?
The rabble starlings roar upon
Trafalgar. The man-eating British lion
By a pimply age brought down.
Here's his head mounted, though only in rhymes,
Beside the head of the last English
Wolf (those starved gloomy times!)
And the last sturgeon of Thames.

THE VOYAGE

Without hope move my words and looks
Toward you, to claim
Neither known face nor held name—
Death-bed, book might keep those. The whole sea's

Accumulations and changes
Are the sea. The sea's elsewhere
Than surrenders to sand and rocks,
Other than men taste who drown out there.

RELIC

I found this jawbone at the sea's edge:
There, crabs, dogfish, broken by the breakers or tossed
To flap for half an hour and turn to a crust
Continue the beginning. The deeps are cold:
In that darkness camaraderie does not hold:
Nothing touches but, clutching, devours. And the jaws,
Before they are satisfied or their stretched purpose
Slacken, go down jaws; go gnawn bare. Jaws
Eat and are finished and the jawbone comes to the beach:
This is the sea's achievement; with shells,
Vertebrae, claws, carapaces, skulls.

Time in the sea eats its tail, thrives, casts these
Indigestibles, the spars of purposes
That failed far from the surface. None grow rich
In the sea. This curved jawbone did not laugh
But gripped, gripped and is now a cenotaph.

WILFRED OWEN'S PHOTOGRAPHS

When Parnell's Irish in the House
Pressed that the British Navy's cat-
O-nine-tails be abolished, what
Shut against them? It was
Neither Irish nor English nor of that
Decade, but of the species.

Predictably, Parliament
Squared against the motion. As soon
Let the old school tie be rent
Off their necks, and give thanks, as see gone
No shame but a monument—
Trafalgar not better known.

"To discontinue it were as much
As ship not powder and cannonballs
But brandy and women" (Laughter). Hearing which
A witty profound Irishman calls
For a "cat" into the House, and sits to watch
The gentry fingering its stained tails.

Whereupon . . .
                    quietly, unopposed,
The motion was passed.

AN OTTER

I

Underwater eyes, an eel's
Oil of water body, neither fish nor beast is the otter:
    Four-legged yet water-gifted, to outfish fish;
        With webbed feet and long ruddering tail
        And a round head like an old tomcat.

    Brings the legend of himself
From before wars or burials, in spite of hounds and vermin-
        poles;
    Does not take root like the badger. Wanders, cries;
        Gallops along land he no longer belongs to;
        Re-enters the water by melting.

    Of neither water nor land. Seeking
Some world lost when first he dived, that he cannot come at
        since,
    Takes his changed body into the holes of lakes;
        As if blind, cleaves the stream's push till he licks
        The pebbles of the source; from sea

    To sea crosses in three nights
Like a king in hiding. Crying to the old shape of the starlit
        land,
    Over sunken farms where the bats go round,
        Without answer. Till light and birdsong come
        Walloping up roads with the milk wagon.

The hunt's lost him. Pads on mud,
Among sedges, nostrils a surface bead,
The otter remains, hours. The air,
Circling the globe, tainted and necessary,

Mingling tobacco-smoke, hounds and parsley,
Comes carefully to the sunk lungs.
So the self under the eye lies,
Attendant and withdrawn. The otter belongs

In double robbery and concealment—
From water that nourishes and drowns, and from land
That gave him his length and the mouth of the hound.
He keeps fat in the limpid integument

Reflections live on. The heart beats thick,
Big trout muscle out of the dead cold;
Blood is the belly of logic; he will lick
The fishbone bare. And can take stolen hold

On a bitch otter in a field full
Of nervous horses, but linger nowhere.
Yanked above hounds, reverts to nothing at all,
To this long pelt over the back of a chair.

WITCHES

Once was every woman the witch
To ride a weed the ragwort road;
Devil to do whatever she would:
Each rosebud, every old bitch.

Did they bargain their bodies or no?
Proprietary the devil that
Went horsing on their every thought
When they scowled the strong and lucky low.

Dancing in Ireland nightly, gone
To Norway (the ploughboy bridled),
Nightlong under the blackamoor spraddled,
Back beside their spouse by dawn

As if they had dreamed all. Did they dream it?
Oh, our science says they did.
It was all wishfully dreamed in bed.
Small psychology would unseam it.

Bitches still sulk, rosebuds blow,
And we are devilled. And though these weep
Over our harms, who's to know
Where their feet dance while their heads sleep?

NOVEMBER

The month of the drowned dog. After long rain the land
Was sodden as the bed of an ancient lake,
Treed with iron and birdless. In the sunk lane
The ditch—a seep silent all summer—

Made brown foam with a big voice: that, and my boots
On the lane's scrubbed stones, in the gulleyed leaves,
Against the hill's hanging silence;
Mist silvering the droplets on the bare thorns

Slower than the change of daylight.
In a let of the ditch a tramp was bundled asleep:
Face tucked down into beard, drawn in
Under its hair like a hedgehog's. I took him for dead,

But his stillness separated from the death
Of the rotting grass and the ground. A wind chilled,
And a fresh comfort tightened through him,
Each hand stuffed deeper into the other sleeve.

His ankles, bound with sacking and hairy band,
Rubbed each other, resettling. The wind hardened;
A puff shook a glittering from the thorns,
And again the rains' dragging grey columns

Smudged the farms. In a moment
The fields were jumping and smoking; the thorns
Quivered, riddled with the glassy verticals.
I stayed on under the welding cold

D 49

Watching the tramp's face glisten and the drops on his coat
Flash and darken. I thought what strong trust
Slept in him—as the trickling furrows slept,
And the thorn-roots in their grip on darkness;

And the buried stones, taking the weight of winter;
The hill where the hare crouched with clenched teeth.
Rain plastered the land till it was shining
Like hammered lead, and I ran, and in the rushing wood

Shuttered by a black oak leaned.
The keeper's gibbet had owls and hawks
By the neck, weasels, a gang of cats, crows:
Some, stiff, weightless, twirled like dry bark bits

In the drilling rain. Some still had their shape,
Had their pride with it; hung, chins on chests,
Patient to outwait these worst days that beat
Their crowns bare and dripped from their feet.

THE PERFECT FORMS

Here is Socrates, born under Pisces,
Smiling, complacent as a phallus,
Or Buddha, whose one thought fills immensity:

Visage of Priapus: the undying tail-swinging
Stupidity of the donkey
That carries Christ. How carefully he nurses

This six-day abortion of the Absolute—
No better for the fosterings
Of fish, reptile and tree-leaper throughout

Their ages of Godforsaken darkness—
This monstrous-headed difficult child!
Of such is the kingdom of heaven.

THRUSHES

Terrifying are the attent sleek thrushes on the lawn,
More coiled steel than living—a poised
Dark deadly eye, those delicate legs
Triggered to stirrings beyond sense—with a start, a bounce, a
    stab
Overtake the instant and drag out some writhing thing.
No indolent procrastinations and no yawning stares,
No sighs or head-scratchings. Nothing but bounce and stab
And a ravening second.

Is it their single-mind-sized skulls, or a trained
Body, or genius, or a nestful of brats
Gives their days this bullet and automatic
Purpose? Mozart's brain had it, and the shark's mouth
That hungers down the blood-smell even to a leak of its own
Side and devouring of itself: efficiency which
Strikes too streamlined for any doubt to pluck at it
Or obstruction deflect.

With a man it is otherwise. Heroisms on horseback,
Outstripping his desk-diary at a broad desk,
Carving at a tiny ivory ornament
For years: his act worships itself—while for him,
Though he bends to be blent in the prayer, how loud and
    above what
Furious spaces of fire do the distracting devils
Orgy and hosannah, under what wilderness
Of black silent waters weep.

SINGERS

The dregs of a long drinking sit late
Sinking far from their glasses, a grim
Unison not to be put out
By calendar more than by clock: they have come

To the lord who abducted the miller's daughter,
The farmer who killed his wife and a king—
One thrust. By Guinness, by mild, by bitter
Those stunned unspigotted heads sing,

Rightly too, the drunkenness of time:
For the words of all headache to come,
Of all gone, are on Dick, Jack, Dan,
And a curse on the age that loses the tune.

BULLFROG

With their lithe long strong legs
Some frogs are able
To thump upon double-
Bass strings though pond-water deadens and clogs.

But you, bullfrog, you pump out
Whole fogs full of horn—a threat
As of a liner looming. True
That, first hearing you
Disgorging your gouts of darkness like a wounded god,
Not utterly fantastical I expected
(As in some antique tale depicted)
A broken-down bull up to its belly in mud,
Sucking black swamp up, belching out black cloud

And a squall of gudgeon and lilies.
                                                    A surprise,
To see you, a boy's prize,
No bigger than a rat—all dumb silence
In your little old woman hands.

CRAG JACK'S APOSTASY

The churches, lord, all the dark churches
Stooped over my cradle once:
I came clear, but my god's down
Under the weight of all that stone:
Both my power and my luck since
Have kicked at the world and slept in ditches.

I do not desire to change my ways,
But now call continually
On you, god or not god, who
Come to my sleeping body through
The world under the world; pray
That I may see more than your eyes

In an animal's dreamed head; that I shall—
Waking, dragged suddenly
From a choir-shaken height
By the world, lord, and its dayfall—
Keep more than the memory
Of a wolf's head, of eagles' feet.

PIKE

Pike, three inches long, perfect
Pike in all parts, green tigering the gold.
Killers from the egg: the malevolent aged grin.
They dance on the surface among the flies.

Or move, stunned by their own grandeur,
Over a bed of emerald, silhouette
Of submarine delicacy and horror.
A hundred feet long in their world.

In ponds, under the heat-struck lily pads—
Gloom of their stillness:
Logged on last year's black leaves, watching upwards.
Or hung in an amber cavern of weeds

The jaws' hooked clamp and fangs
Not to be changed at this date;
A life subdued to its instrument;
The gills kneading quietly, and the pectorals.

Three we kept behind glass,
Jungled in weed: three inches, four,
And four and a half: fed fry to them—
Suddenly there were two. Finally one

With a sag belly and the grin it was born with.
And indeed they spare nobody.
Two, six pounds each, over two feet long,
High and dry and dead in the willow-herb —

One jammed past its gills down the other's gullet:
The outside eye stared: as a vice locks—
The same iron in this eye
Though its film shrank in death.

A pond I fished, fifty yards across,
Whose lilies and muscular tench
Had outlasted every visible stone
Of the monastery that planted them—

Stilled legendary depth:
It was as deep as England. It held
Pike too immense to stir, so immense and old
That past nightfall I dared not cast

But silently cast and fished
With the hair frozen on my head
For what might move, for what eye might move.
The still splashes on the dark pond,

Owls hushing the floating woods
Frail on my ear against the dream
Darkness beneath night's darkness had freed,
That rose slowly towards me, watching.

SNOWDROP

Now is the globe shrunk tight
Round the mouse's dulled wintering heart.
Weasel and crow, as if moulded in brass,
Move through an outer darkness
Not in their right minds,
With the other deaths. She, too, pursues her ends,
Brutal as the stars of this month,
Her pale head heavy as metal.

SUNSTROKE

Frightening the blood in its tunnel
The mowing machine ate at the field of grass.

My eyes had been glared dark. Through a red heat
The cradled guns, damascus, blued, flared—

At every stir sliding their molten embers
Into my head. Sleekly the clover

Bowed and flowed backward
Over the saw-set swimming blades

Till the blades bit—roots, stones, ripped into red—
Some baby's body smoking among the stalks.

Reek of paraffin oil and creosote
Swabbing my lungs doctored me back

Laid on a sack in the great-beamed engine-shed.
I drank at stone, at iron of plough and harrow;

Dulled in a pit, heard thick walls of rain
And voices in swaddled confinement near me

Warm as veins. I lay healing
Under the ragged length of a dog fox

That dangled head downward from one of the beams,
With eyes open, forepaws strained at a leap—

Also surprised by the rain.

59

CLEOPATRA TO THE ASP

The bright mirror I braved: the devil in it
Loved me like my soul, my soul:
Now that I seek myself in a serpent
My smile is fatal.

Nile moves in me; my thighs splay
Into the squalled Mediterranean;
My brain hides in that Abyssinia
Lost armies foundered towards.

Desert and river unwrinkle again.
Seeming to bring them the waters that make drunk
Caesar, Pompey, Antony I drank.
Now let the snake reign.

A half-deity out of Capricorn,
This rigid Augustus mounts
With his sword virginal indeed; and has shorn
Summarily the moon-horned river

From my bed. May the moon
Ruin him with virginity! Drink me, now, whole
With coiled Egypt's past; then from my delta
Swim like a fish toward Rome.

LUPERCALIA

1

The dog loved its churlish life,
Scraps, thefts. Its declined blood
An anarchy of mindless pride.
Nobody's pet, but good enough

To double with a bitch as poor.
It had bitten ears and little stone eyes,
A mouth like an incinerator.
It held man's reasonable ways

Between its teeth. Received death
Closed eyes and grinning mouth.

2

This woman's as from death's touch: a surviving
Barrenness: she abides; perfect,
But flung from the wheel of the living,
The past killed in her, the future plucked out.

The dead are indifferent underground.
Little the live may learn from them—
A sort of hair and bone wisdom,
A worn witchcraft accoutrement

Of proverbs. Now the brute's quick
Be tinder: old spark of the blood-heat
And not death's touch engross her bed,
Though that has stripped her stark indeed.

3

Goats, black, not angels, but
Bellies round as filled wine-skins
Slung under carcase bones.
Yet that's no brute light

And no merely mountain light—
Their eyes' golden element.
Rustle of their dry hooves, dry patter,
Wind in the oak-leaves; and their bent

Horns, stamp, sudden reared stare
Startle women. Spirit of the ivy,
Stink of goat, of a rank thriving,
O mountain listener.

4

Over sand that the sun's burned out
Thudding feet of the powerful,
Their oiled bodies brass-bright
In a drift of dust. The earth's crammed full,

Its baked red bellying to the sky's
Electric blue. Their attitudes—
A theorem of flung effort, blades:
Nothing mortal falters their poise

Though wet with blood: the dog has blessed
Their fury. Fresh thongs of goat-skin
In their hands they go bounding past,
And deliberate welts have snatched her in

To the figure of racers. Maker of the world,
Hurrying the lit ghost of man
Age to age while the body hold,
Touch this frozen one.

Ted Hughes's first volume, *The Hawk in the Rain*—a choice of the Poetry Book Society and Winner of the first Publication Award in a contest sponsored by the New York City Poetry Centre—was generally acclaimed as one of the most interesting and most important first volumes of verse to have appeared for a considerable time.

Lupercal will, we are confident, justify and confirm the predictions made about Mr Hughes's stature, ability and promise. It is distinguished by all the virtues of its predecessor; and it is notable, too, for a remarkable growth in poetic skill and maturity.